Hard Freight

THE WESLEYAN POETRY PROGRAM: VOLUME 69

HARD
FREIGHT
by

CHARLES WRIGHT

WESLEYAN UNIVERSITY PRESS

Middletown, Connecticut

Acknowledgement is gratefully made to The Golem Press of Santa Ana, California, and to the following periodical journals, in the pages of which some of the poems in this book were first published: *Crazy Horse, Granite, Hearse, The Iowa Review, Lillabulero, Poetry, Ploughshares, The Seneca Review, Skywriting, The Southern Review* and *West Coast Poetry Review*.

The poems 'Blackwater Mountain', 'Chinoiserie', 'Clinchfield Station', 'Congenital', 'Dog Creek Mainline', 'Entries', 'Epithalamion', 'The Fever Toy', 'Negatives', 'Nightdream', 'Nightletter', 'Northhanger Ridge', 'Nouns', 'Portrait of the Poet in Abraham von Werdt's Dream' and 'Victory Garden' were first published in *Poetry*.

The poems 'Definitions', 'Firstborn', 'The New Poem', 'Nocturne', 'Notes for Oscar Wilde at San Miniato', 'One Two Three' and 'Oscar Wilde at San Miniato' first appeared in *The Venice Notebook*, published by the Barn Dream Press of Boston in 1971.

Library of Congress Cataloging in Publication Data
Wright, Charles, 1935–
    Hard freight.

    (The Wesleyan poetry program, v. 69)
    Poems.
    Includes bibliographical references.
    I. Title.
PS3573.R52H3   811'5'4   73–6014
ISBN 0-8195-2069-1
ISBN 0-8195-1069-6 (pbk.)

Manufactured in the United States of America
First edition

For my Mother and Father

What is the use of talking, and there is no end of talking,
There is no end of things in the heart.
                                              —EP/Rihaku

CONTENTS

End-papers

Homages

HOMAGE TO EZRA POUND

Past San Sebastiano, past
The Ogni Santi and San Trovaso, down
The Zattere and left
Across the tiered bridge to where
— Off to the right, half-hidden —
The Old Dogana burns in the spring sun:
This is how you arrive.

This is the street where Pound lives,
A cul-de-sac
Of rheumy corners and cracked stone,
At whose approach the waters
Assemble, the gulls cry out:
In here — unspeaking, unturned — he waits,
Sifting the cold affections of the blood.

※

Others have led the way,
Vanishing in their sleep, their beds
Unmade, the sheets still damp
From what has set them apart —
Cancer or bad lungs, the wrack
Of advancing age, the dull
Incense of suicide . . .

And he has survived,
Or refused to follow, and now
Walks in the slow strobe of the sunlight,
Or sits in his muffled rooms,
Wondering where it went bad,
And leans to the signal, the low
Rustle of wings, the splash of an oar.

※

Today is one of those days
One swears is a prophesy:
The air explicit and moist,
As though filled with unanswered prayers;
The twilight, starting to slide
Its sooty fingers along the trees;
And you, Pound,

Awash in the wrong life,
Cut loose upon the lagoon (the wind
Off-shore, and gaining), the tide going out . . .
Here is your caul and caustic,
Here is your garment,
Cold-blooded father of light —
Rise and be whole again.

Venice

HOMAGE TO ARTHUR RIMBAUD

Laying our eggs like moths
In the cold cracks of your eyes,
Brushing your hands with our dark wings

— Desperate to attempt
An entrance, to touch that light
Which buoys you like a flame,
That it might warm our own lives —,

We cluster about your death
As though it were reachable.

For almost a hundred years
We've gathered outside your legend (and been afraid
Of what such brilliance affords;

And knew the while you were risen, your flight
Pneumatic and pure, invisible as a fever;
And knew the flight was forever,
Leaving us what we deserve:

Syllables, flowers, black ice;
The exit, the split cocoon . . .

Charleville

HOMAGE TO BARON CORVO

Of all the poses, of all the roles,
This is the one I keep: you pass
On the canal, your pope's robes
Aflame in a secret light, the four
Oars of your gondola white
As moth wings in the broken dark,
The quail-eyed fisher-boys
Sliding the craft like a coffin out to sea;
The air grows hard; the boat's wake
Settles behind you like a wasted breath.

　　　　　°

(For months, Corvo, you floated through my sleep
As I tried to track you down:
That winter you lived in a doorway;
The days and nights on these back canals
You spent in a musty blanket,
Your boat both bed and refuge —
And writing always
The book, the indescribable letters . . .
Was it the vengeance only
That kept you alive, the ripe corkscrew
Twisted and deep in the bottle's throat?

One afternoon — in the late spring — I went
To San Michele, to see
The sealed drawer that holds your name,
To take you flowers, as one
Is moved to do for the dead, and found
Not even a vase to put them in.
Leaving, I spread them on the lagoon,

Ungraftable shoots of blood. There is, you said,
A collusion of things in this world . . .)

❀

And so you escape. What books there are,
Old hustler, will never exhume you,
Nor places you stayed.
Hadrian, Nicholas Crabbe, you hide
Where the dust hides now,
Your con with its last trick turned,
Stone nightmare come round again —
Fadeout: your boat, Baron, edges
Toward the horizon, a sky where toads,
Their eyes new fire,
Alone at the landings blink and blink.

Venice

HOMAGE TO X

The red earth, the light diffuse
In the flat-leaved limbs of the trees;
A cold, perpetual rain
As though from a heaving breast;
O loved ones, O angels . . .

           ✿

The thing, as always, begins
In transit, the water infusion
Oily and phosphorescent —
The vine is a blue light,
The cup is a star.

           ✿

In the dream you will see a city,
Foreign and repetitious,
The plants unspeakably green;
This is of no concern; your job
Is the dust, the belly-relinquishing dust.

           ✿

It's the day before yesterday,
It's the other side of the sky:
The body that bears your number
Will not be new, will not be your own
And will not remember your name.

Prague / Prague-Strashnitz

Hard Freight

THE NEW POEM

It will not resemble the sea.
It will not have dirt on its thick hands.
It will not be part of the weather.

It will not reveal its name.
It will not have dreams you can count on.
It will not be photogenic.

It will not attend our sorrow.
It will not console our children.
It will not be able to help us.

PORTRAIT OF THE POET
IN ABRAHAM VON WERDT'S DREAM

Outside, the Venice skyline, and stars
Half-seen through an opened window;
Inside, it's the Renaissance,
The men in hose,
The furnishings elegant, but spare;
A griffin rears in the archway;
An eagle dives from the ceiling;
And over the far wall — like Dürer's —
Two cherubs support the three
Disordered initials of my signature.

Paper is stacked in neat piles, as I
First drew them; square blocks of type, their beds
Tilted and raised, their letters reversed,
Glisten among the shadows;
Two men in the foreground work
A press, inking and setting; a third
Is washing his hands, kneeling
In front of a tub; a fourth, his right arm
Extended, adjusts the unused type;
A fifth is correcting proof.

Alone in an alcove, a sixth man, unnoticed
And unfamiliar, his strange clothes
Centuries out of date, is writing, his back turned
To what I tried to record.
The lines, a spidery darkness, move
Across the page. Now
He looks this way. And now he rises
— XYZ, his mouth says, XYZ —,
Thrusting the paper into my hands.
These words are the words he has written.

CHINOISERIE

Why not? The mouths of the ginger blooms slide open,
The willows drag their knuckles across the earth;
Each year has its fields that no one tends.

Our days, unlike the long gasps of the wind,
Stay half in love with the rushes, and half with the water reeds.
Outside the body, all things are encumbrances.

WHITE

Carafe, compotier, sea shell, vase:
Blank spaces, white objects;
Luminous knots along the black rope.

✿

The clouds, great piles of oblivion, cruise
Over the world, the wind at their backs
Forever. They darken whomever they please.

✿

The angel, his left hand on your left shoulder;
The bones, in draped white, at the door;
The bed-sheets, the pillow-case; your eyes.

✿

I write your name for the last time in this mist,
White breath on the windowpane,
And watch it vanish. No, it stays there.

✿

White, and the leaf clicks; dry rock;
White, and the wave spills.
Dogwood, the stripe, headlights, teeth.

22

DEFINITIONS

The blades of the dwarf palm,
Honing themselves in the wind;
The ice plant, blistering red along
Its green, immaculate skin;
The moon, sad marigold, drooping
On dark, attenuant waters . . .

Such images quicken you,
Suspended impurities
Caught in the night's sieve,
Far beyond any worth
They might possess or define,
Disjunctive edges of things.

Offering little hope, no consolation,
Each, in its own way, is
Something indelicate, and cold,
Something to listen for —
A scar, fat worm, which feeds at the lungs;
A cough, the blood in the handkerchief.

ONE TWO THREE

A shift in the wind the darkness
Beading about your eyelids
The sour pull of the blood
Everything works against you
The way the evening comes down
Its trellises one rose at a time
The watery knots of light
That lap at your memory
The way you thought of your life once
An endless falling of seeds

        ✿

Already places exist
Which cannot reshelter you
Hands you have clasped for the last time
Familiar mirrors remain
That will not contain your face
Words you have uttered
That will not remember your tongue
The sofas that held your sleep
Gradually rise to assume
Their untouched shapes and their dreams

        ✿

The wave will deliver you
Your arms thrown out like driftwood the shore
Eroding away at your touch
Your fingers ingrained in its loose skin
The idea of absence
Sprouting like grass from your side
Your autobiography

Completed no less than what
Always you claimed it would be the stone
That no one will roll away

NOUNS

Nouns are precise, they wear
The boots of authority;

Nouns are not easily pleased.
Nouns are assured, they know

Whom to precede and whom to follow,
They know what dependence means,

That touchstone of happiness;
They need no apologist.

When nouns fall to disuse, and die,
Their bones do not coalesce.

Such absences implicate
No person, no place, no thing.

FIRSTBORN

— Omnia quae sunt, lumina sunt —

1.

The sugar dripping into your vein;
The jaundice rising upon your face like a blush;
The glass box they keep you in —

The bandage over your eyes;
The curdled milk on your lips;
The plastic tube in your throat —

The unseen hands that linger against your skin;
The name, like a new scar, at your wrist;
The glass box they keep you in —

We bring what we have to bring;
We give what we have to give;
Welcome, sweet Luke, to your life.

2.

The bougainvillaea's redress
Pulses throughout the hillside, its slow
Network of vines

Holding the earth together, giving it breath;
Outside your window, hibiscus and columbine
Tend to their various needs;

The summer enlarges.
                              You, too, enlarge,
Becoming accessible,
Your liquid reshufflings

Protracted and ill defined,
Yet absolute after all, the new skin
Blossoming pink and clear.

3.

You lie here beside me now,
Ineffable, elsewhere still.
What should one say to a son?

Emotions and points of view, the large
Abstractions we like to think
We live by — or would live by if things

Were other than what they are;
Or we were; or others were;
If all were altered and more distinct?

Or something immediate,
Descriptive, the virtuous use of words?
What can one say to a son?

4.

If it were possible, if
A way had been overlooked
To pull that rib of pure light

Out of its cage, those few felicitous vowels
Which expiate everything . . .
But nothing has been left out,

Nothing been overlooked.
The words remain in the dark, and will
Continue to glitter there;

No tricks we try to invent,
No strategies, can now extract them.
And dust is dust for a long time.

5.

What I am trying to say
Is this — I tell you, only, the thing
That I have come to believe:

Indenture yourself to the land;
Imagine you touch its raw edges
In all weather, time and again;

Imagine its colors; try
To imitate, day by day,
The morning's growth and the dusk,

The movement of all their creatures;
Surrender yourself, and be glad;
This is the law that endures.

6.

The foothills of Tennessee,
The mountains of North Carolina,
Their rivers and villages

— Hiwassee and Cherokee,
The Cumberland, Pisgah and Nantahala,
Unaka and Unicoi —

Brindle and sing in your blood;
Their sounds are the sounds you hear,
Their shapes are the shapes you see

Regardless, whenever you concentrate
Upon the remembered earth
— All things that are are lights.

SLIDES OF VERONA

1. Here where Catullus sat like snow
   Over the Adige the blooms drift
   West on the west-drifting wind

2. Cangrande mellifluous ghost sails
   His stone boat above the yard

3. St George and Trebizond each
   Elsewhere still hold their poses still burn

4. Death with its long tongue licks
   Mastino's hand affection he thinks
   Such sweetness such loyalty

5. Here comes Whatever Will Come
   His shoulders hunched under lost luggage

6. Two men their necks broken hang
   Opposite where the hill once was
   And that's where the rainbow ends

7. The star of the jasmine plant
   Who follows you now who leads

8. The great gates like wings unfold
   The angel gives him a push
   The rosaries click like locks

9. White glove immaculate touch
   How cold you are how quiet

GRACE

Its hair is a fine weed,
Matted, where something has lain,
Or fallen repeatedly:

Its arms are rivers that sink
Suddenly under the earth,
Elbow and wristbone: cold sleeve:

Its face is a long soliloquy,
A language of numerals,
Impossible to erase.

NEGATIVES

This is the light we dream in,
The milk light of midnight, the full moon
Reversing the balance like shapes on a negative:
The chalk hills, the spectral sky,
The black rose in flame,
Its odors and glittery hooks
Waiting for something to snag.

The mulberries wink like dimes;
Fat sheep, the mesquite and chaparral   *C A ?*
Graze at their own sweet speed,
The earth white sugar;
Two miles below, and out,
The surf has nothing to add.

— Is this what awaits us, amorphous
Cobalt and zinc, a wide tide
Of brilliance we cannot define
Or use, and leafless, without guilt;
No guidelines or flutter, no
Cadence to pinpoint, no no?

Silence. As though the doorway behind
Us were liquid, were black water;
As though we might enter; as though
The ferry were there,
Ready to take us across,
— Remembering now, unwatermarked —
The blackout like scarves in our new hair.

EMBLEMS

Winds cross, stars unhood, the clouds
Are rivers beneath the sky:
Chaos, the inked-in valley.
— It is an apple, a disc, a target with rings

(Whose hand relinquishes it
— His robe like puddles about his feet —
Is braceleted, long of nail.
It is a circle. Take it).

Fig. 1

These small mouths blow black air, these hands
In supplication extend
Beyond the curtain of light. If this horn
Can make the hooves

Of these four horses dance, can make
Their riders balance longsword and scythe,
The bodies beneath them start to rise,
Then music it is, sweet music.

Fig. 2

THE FEVER TOY

The arms seem clumsy at first,
Outsize, the eyes detached; at odd angles,
The wrists respond to no touch;
Rickety, flat-veined, the legs
Push out like stems from their bulbous feet;
The fingers repeat themselves.

What pleasure this gives, this sure
Mating of parts, this slip and catch
Of bone to bone, of stiff flesh
To socket and joint, this gift
You give yourself in advance.
Instructions are not enclosed, and yet

How well you assemble it,
How well you insert yourself in each
Corner and crevice of its wrong arms:
Its breath caresses your eyes,
Its lips — like larvae — explore your face,
Its lashes become your own.

And this is how it begins.
This is the way your true name
Returns and returns again,
Your sorrow becoming a foreign tongue,
Your body becoming a foreign tongue,
Blue idiom, blue embrace.

THE OTHER SIDE

I come to the great noose of water;
Like stone gods, the succorers wait,
Dressed in their tiny garments. All day
They stare from the opposite shore.

The boughs of the Manchineel
Let fall their blindness and black apples.
Gratefully I undress. The first stone
Rises like light to my hand.

NOTES FOR OSCAR WILDE AT SAN MINIATO

1.

These wings of clear flame (like dying fires,
Like vanishing wakes,
The lost light
Down there — the river? — grotesque, . . .

2.

Florence: a vortex, a mouth,
Vertiginous hive . . .

NOCTURNE

Florence, verticillate throat,
A hiss of enfolding wings,
The tortuous river enflamed,
The water like scales in the fire's flare . . .

3.

The fire's wings, the cries,
The long wakes of ever-diminishing light;
Below, grotesque and wide, the river
Flashes and burns like a snake;
The sudden faces of thieves, their laughter;
I stand, on San Miniato's steps,
Between two cypress, two wicks,
Two guttered and useless flames . . .

— After Dino Campana

OSCAR WILDE AT SAN MINIATO

Unnatural city, monastic transparency,
Below me (in flames, the tide-lines of light
Lapping the night's brim)
You sift your impossible loves,
Your rich, suicidal dreams.
Beside the steps where I climb, four youths,
Mocking and drunk with scorn,
Flip their invisible coins.
The river flashes and winks.
Insatiable disillusion,
Dark ship, I watch the candescent fevers rise
Which burn you, rise and reflare.
Black hull, your bodies are burning like lamps,
Their bones death's rattle under the lunar fire.

— After Dino Campana

NOCTURNE

Florence, abyss of enfolding light:

❋

The tram-lines, like wings of fire —
Their long, retreating sparks, their susurrant cries:

❋

The Arno, glittering snake, touches
The white cloisters of flame, easing
Its burden, the chill of its scales:

❋

The double cypress, extinguished theories
Harsher than hedgerows, harsher
Than alms-boxes; harsher, too,
Than songs my pandering heart
Continues to sing, snatches of melody:

❋

— I love the old-fashioned whores
Swollen with sperm
Who plop, like enormous toads, on all fours
Over the featherbed
And wait, and puff, and snort,
Flaccid as any bellows —:

❋

&c. &c. &c. &c. &c. &c. &c. &c. &c. &c.

— After Dino Campana

41

YELLOW

Yellow is for regret, the distal, the second hand:
The grasshopper's wing, that yellow, the slur of dust;
Back light, the yellow of loneliness;
The yellow of animals, their yellow eyes;
The holy yellow of death;
Intuitive yellow, the yellow of air;
The double yellow, telling who comes and who goes;
The yellow of yellowhammers, one drop of the devil's blood;
The yellow of what is past;
Yellow of wormwood, yellow of straw;
The yellow of circuits, the yellow beneath the skin;
The yellow of pencils, their black veins;
Amaranth yellow, bright bloom;
The yellow of sulfur, the finger, the road home.

DOG CREEK MAINLINE

Dog Creek: cat track and bird splay,
Spindrift and windfall; woodrot;
Odor of muscadine, the blue creep
Of kingsnake and copperhead;
Nightweed; frog spit and floating heart,
Backwash and snag pool: Dog Creek

Starts in the leaf reach and shoal run of the blood;
Starts in the falling light just back
Of the fingertips; starts
Forever in the black throat
You ask redemption of, in wants
You waken to, the odd door:

Its sky, old empty valise,
Stands open, departure in mind; its three streets,
Y-shaped and brown,
Go up the hills like a fever;
Its houses link and deploy
— This ointment, false flesh in another color.

☙

Five cutouts, five silhouettes
Against the American twilight; the year
Is 1941; remembered names
— Rosendale, Perry and Smith —
Rise like dust in the deaf air;
The tops spin, the poison swells in the arm:

The trees in their jade death-suits,
The birds with their opal feet,
Shimmer and weave on the shoreline;

The moths, like forget-me-nots, blow
Up from the earth, their wet teeth
Breaking the dark, the raw grain;

The lake in its cradle hums
The old songs: out of its ooze, their heads
Like tomahawks, the turtles ascend
And settle back, leaving their chill breath
In blisters along the bank;
Locked in their wide drawer, the pike lie still as knives.

        *

Hard freight. It's hard freight
From Ducktown to Copper Hill, from Six
To Piled High: Dog Creek is on this line,
Indigent spur; cross-tie by cross-tie it takes
You back, the red wind
Caught at your neck like a prize:

(The heart is a hieroglyph;
The fingers, like praying mantises, poise
Over what they have once loved;
The ear, cold cave, is an absence,
Tapping its own thin wires;
The eye turns in on itself.

The tongue is a white water.
In its slick ceremonies the light
Gathers, and is refracted, and moves
Outward, over the lips,
Over the dry skin of the world.
The tongue is a white water.).

BACKTRACK

— JB, H & Mr B

This is the death of water, the sky gone bad;
This is the wall of blurred names;
This is the drop of wax, the shined shoe;
This is the noise, the wardrobe of no address —

And this is the shirt, bone shirt, chalk and chalk dust,
Its coat, black rainbow, reracked, its cuffs
Shot back, its buttons loose flake
That flash and over the hung earth hang.

SKY VALLEY RIDER

Same place, same auto-da-fe:
Late August, the air replete, the leaves
Grotesque in their limp splendor,
The dust like guilt on the window sills,
On the pressed pants of suits
Hung like meat on their black hooks:

I walked these roads once, two steps
Behind my own life, my pockets stuffed with receipts
For goods I'd never asked for:
Complacency, blind regret; belief;
Compassion I recognized in the left palm;
Respect, slick stick, in the right:

One I have squandered, one
I have sloughed like a cracked skin; the others,
Small charms against an eventual present,
I keep in the camphor box
Beside my handkerchiefs, the slow roll
Of how I'll unravel, signatures.

         ❁

The tinkly hymns, the wrong songs:
This one's for you, 15, lost
On the wide waters that circle beneath the earth;
You touched me once, but not now,
Your fingers like blue streamers, the stump
Of your hand, perhaps, in time to that music still:

Down by the haying shed, the white pines
Commence with their broomy sounds;
The orchard, the skeletal trunks on Anne's Ridge

— Stone and stone-colored cloud —
Gather the light and hold fast;
Two thousand acres of loneliness:

Leaf over leaf, the green sky:
Sycamore, black gum, oak, ash;
Wind-scythe at work in the far fields;
In the near, plum-flame of larkspur:
Whatever has been, remains —
Fox fire, pale semaphore in the skull's night.

❉

The past, wrecked accordion, plays on, its one tune
My song, its one breath my breath,
The square root, the indivisible cipher . . .

SEX

The Holston lolls like a tongue here, its banks
Gummy and ill at ease; across the state line,
Moccasin Gap declines in a leafy sneer.
Darkness, the old voyeur, moistens his chapped lips.

Unnoticed by you, of course, your mind
Elsewhere and groping: *the stuck clasp, her knees,*
The circle around the moon, O anything . . .
— Black boat you step from, the wet's slow sift.

Then Nothing, sleek fish, nuzzles the surface calm.
The fireflies drag and relight.
The wound is unwound, the flash is tipped on the fuse,
And on the long, long waters of What's Left.

BLACKWATER MOUNTAIN

That time of evening, weightless and disparate,
When the loon cries, when the small bass
Jostle the lake's reflections, when
The green of the oak begins
To open its robes to the dark, the green
Of water to offer itself to the flames,
When lily and lily pad
Husband the last light
Which flares like a white disease, then disappears:
This is what I remember. And this:

The slap of the jacklight on the cove;
The freeze-frame of ducks
Below us; your shots; the wounded flop
And skid of one bird to the thick brush;
The moon of your face in the fire's glow;
The cold; the darkness. Young,
Wanting approval, what else could I do?
And did, for two hours, waist-deep in the lake,
The thicket as black as death,
Without success or reprieve, try.

The stars over Blackwater Mountain
Still dangle and flash like hooks, and ducks
Coast on the evening water;
The foliage is like applause.
I stand where we stood before and aim
My flashlight down to the lake. A black duck
Explodes to my right, hangs, and is gone.
He shows me the way to you;
He shows me the way to a different fire
Where you, black moon, warm your hands.

VICTORY GARDEN

Blue agony of the morning-glory;
The fuchsia's psoriasis;
These flowers unscab the heart. Sick skin, sick skin.
Pus flares in the daisy chain.

The pomegranate, its red chambers
In ruin, its seeds like grubs in the earth's side,
Feels nothing of this, nor cares.
In the salt wind, its leaves rekindle and rain.

NORTHHANGER RIDGE

Half-bridge over nothingness,
White sky of the palette knife; blot orange,
Vertical blacks; blue, birdlike,
Drifting up from the next life,
The heat-waves, like consolation, wince —
One cloud, like a trunk, stays shut
Above the horizon; off to the left, dream-wires,
Hill-snout like a crocodile's.

Or so I remember it,
Their clenched teeth in their clenched mouths,
Their voices like shards of light,
Brittle, unnecessary.
Ruined shoes, roots, the cabinet of lost things:
This is the same story,
Its lips in flame, its throat a dark water,
The page stripped of its meaning.

                    ✿

Sunday, and Father Dog is turned loose:
Up the long road the children's feet
Snick in the dust like raindrops; the wind
Excuses itself and backs off; inside, heat
Lies like a hand on each head;
Slither and cough. Now Father Dog
Addles our misconceptions, points, preens,
His finger a white flag, run up, run down.

Bow-wow and arf, the Great Light;
O, and the Great Yes, and the Great No;
Redemption, the cold kiss of release,
&c.; sentences, sentences.

(Meanwhile, docile as shadows, they stare
From their four corners, looks set:
No glitter escapes
This evangelical masonry.)

✿

Candleflame; vigil and waterflow:
Like dust in the night the prayers rise:
From 6 to 6, under the sick Christ,
The children talk to the nothingness,
Crossrack and wound; the dark room
Burns like a coal, goes
Ash to the touch, ash to the tongue's tip;
Blood turns in the wheel:

Something drops from the leaves; the drugged moon
Twists and turns in its sheets; sweet breath
In a dry corner, the black widow reknits her dream.
Salvation again declines,
And sleeps like a skull in the hard ground,
Nothing for ears, nothing for eyes;
It sleeps as it's always slept, without
Shadow, waiting for nothing.

Bible Camp, 1949

TONGUES

Heart's coal; hinge to the dark door;
Tongue that flicks from this blue hill: sunset:
Snail's track and calf's cover;
The last wipe of expectancy.

✿

Dog-days; black dog in the black sky,
Star-toothed, star-shouldered; spins through the flat night
Forever at heel, his tongue
Predicting good-bye, good-bye.

✿

Pillow on which my head lies, tongue
Of the Great Mouth, savor my sleeplessness;
Let drop, on my inner ear,
Your rattle of gratitude, those furred footfalls.

✿

Burnt tongues of the avocado, burnt
Umbers of half a lifetime;
Procession of glints and sparks, sfumato
Of *no* and *perhaps*; lost lights.

PRIMOGENITURE

The door to the book is closed;
The window which gives on the turned earth is closed;
The highway is closed;
Closed, too, are the waters, their lips sealed;
The door to the grass is closed.

Only the chute stays open,
The ruined chute, entering heaven —
Toehold and handhold, the wind like an accident,
The rain like mosquitoes inside your hair,
You stall still, you suffer it not.

— Rose of the afterlife, black mulch we breathe,
Devolve and restore, raise up:
Fireblight and dead bud; rust; spot;
Sore skin and shot hole:
Rechannel these tissues, hold these hands.

54

NIGHTDREAM

Each day is an iceberg,
Dragging its chill paunch underfoot;
Each night is a tree to hang from.
The wooden knife, the mud rope
You scratch your initials on —
Panoply, panoply.

Up and up from his green grave, your father
Wheels in the wind, split scrap of smoke;
Under him stretch, in one file, Bob's Valley, Bald Knob,
The infinite rectitude
Of all that is past: Ouachita,
Ocoee, the slow slide of the Arkansas.

Listen, the old roads are taking flight;
Like bits of string, they, too,
Rise in the pendulous sky,
Whispering, whispering:
Echo has turned a deaf ear,
The wayside is full of leaves.

Your mother floats from her bed
In slow-motion, her loose gown like a fog
Approaching, offering
Meat; across the room, a hand
Again and again
Rises and falls back, clenching, unclenching.

The chambers you've reached, the stones touched,
All stall and worm to a dot;
Sirens drain through the night; lights
Flick and release; the fields, the wet stumps,

Shed their hair and retire;
The bedroom becomes a rose:

(In Kingsport, beneath the trees,
A Captain is singing Dixie; sons
Dance in their gold suits, clapping their hands;
And mothers and fathers, each
In a soft hat, fill
With dust-dolls their long boxes).

POSTSCRIPT

The way the light falls,
Like a cheap dress on a wrought chair;
The way the night comes on,
Like a black shoe on a bride's foot;
The way the earth fills.

You've come back for the last time,
Smoke of the *bucentoro*, white knot
Of the Orto, hung, loose foil,
In the high air: a lone sail
Blots the Salute, mother of waters . . .

Rolfe, Stravinsky, Diaghilev, Pound:
Sweet meat for the wet earth.
Across the salt marsh, the wind,
Bright bird that she is, sings in the eelgrass.
Her breath is a clear elixir.

Venice

CONGENITAL

Here is where it begins here
In the hawk-light in the quiet
The blue of the shag spruce
Lumescent
               night-rinsed and grand

It ends in the afterdamp the rails
Shinned the saltlamps unworkable
It ends in anatomy
In limp wheels in a wisp of skin

— These hands are my father's hands these eyes
Excessively veined his eyes
Unstill ever-turning
The water the same song and the touch

CLINCHFIELD STATION

The road unwinds like a bandage.
These are the benchmarks:
A letter from Yucatan, a ball,
The chairs of the underlife.

Descent is a fact of speech,
A question of need — lampblack, cold-drill,
A glint in the residue:
Dante explained it, how

It bottoms out, becoming a threshold,
The light like a damp confetti,
The wind an apostrophe, the birds
Stone bone in the smooth-limbed trees.

              ✻

Mums in a vase, flakes in a hope chest:
Father advise us, sift our sins —
Ferry us back and step down;
Dock at the Clinchfield Station:

Our Lady of Knoxville reclines there
On her hard bed; a golf club
Hums in the grass. The days, dry cat tracks, come round,
A silence beneath the leaves:

The way back is always into the earth.
Hornbeam or oak root, the ditch, the glass:
It all comes to the same thing:
A length of chain, a white hand.

SYNOPSIS

The white crow of belief
The finger of speechlessness
The eggshell of solitude

The needle of lethargy
The black glove of reprieve
The toad of anticipation

The spider of nothingness
The damp stone of unknowing
The wasp of forgetfulness

End-papers

NIGHTLETTER

The night is a furrow, a queasy, insistent wound. Heavy
    the flies hang, slow wheel the lingering birds. And
    the needle between the fingers, stitching, stitching?
    Sutures, it wants to say, O, sutures, but finds no edge.

When they fold your skin for a boutonniere, will it flower?
    When they give your tongue to the flames, will the ashes
    speak for themselves? The thing that is not left out
    always is what is missing. Everything's certain.

ENTRIES

— The seepage from what you have killed in one part of your
   life will rise, eventually, through your rooms no matter
   what doors you might try to close.

                              ✿

— Always it is the same dark you touch, wherever you touch, its
   odors, its watery flesh closing about you, spreading
   across your hands like new skin.

                              ✿

— What *does* one say to the mad? They hang from their trees
   like swollen fruit, unwilling to fall, untouched by the
   weather. What meetings can hold them there? What
   candor?

                              ✿

— The shed skin, the broken rind, your life but a catch now
   in your own throat . . .

                              ✿

— So one has to dive, sinking more rapidly than what sinks
   in advance of you: once down, once under it all, the
   quieter it becomes, the less fearful it becomes, the
   quieter it becomes.

CHEROKEE

Listen, I've come to dance on your soul; listen, I've come
to tumble your juices into the earth, to settle your
bones in the earth; listen, I've come to cover your eyes
with black leaves, to load them down with black stones;
listen, you're going to where it is nothing, black coffin
under the hill; listen, the black clay will enter your
mouth, the black clay will lodge in a new land; listen,
I've come to bring you a coffin, black house for a black
country; listen, your soul is starting to shrink; listen,
it won't come back; listen, it's blue.

EPITHALAMION

The kingfisher falls through the dry air — whose eye can stop
    his falling;

The crab, her bones shut tight as a baby's fist, waits under
    water, waits to be opened;

And deer, caged in the ring of a flashlight's glare, their
    veins electric, their hearts cold fire, can neither leave
    nor stay —

These are geographies you must assume, and rearrange, drifting
    into the pocked dream hanging before you like the moon,
    faint as a thumbprint on a window pane, gathering dust . . .

Notes

1. 'Homage to Baron Corvo': Baron Corvo was one of the pseudonyms of Frederick William Rolfe, the author of *Hadrian VII* and *The Desire and Pursuit of the Whole*. Rolfe was born in England in 1860; he died in Venice in 1913.

2. 'Homage to X': The first stanza is composed of various fragments from Franz Kafka's *Diaries*.

3. 'Chinoiserie': The third, fifth and sixth lines are variations of lines from different poems from *The Penguin Book of Chinese Verse*, translated by Robert Kotewall and Norman L. Smith.

4. 'Entries': The last stanza is an adaptation of lines from Kafka's *Diaries*.

5. 'Cherokee': This poem is an adaptation of 'To Destroy Life', one of the sacred formulas of the Cherokee, from *American Indian Poetry*, translated by James Mooney. Blue signified for the Cherokee distress, despair, despondency.